W9-CXO-919

F.A. DAVIS COMPANY
1879-1979

Illustrations by John H. Ott
Edited by John Francis Marion

F.A. DAVIS COMPANY
1879-1979

A *very* personal account
by
Robert H. Craven
President

Library of Congress Cataloging in Publication Data

Craven, Robert H   1922-
  F. A. Davis Company, 1879-1979.

  Includes bibliographical references.
   1. Craven, Robert H., 1922-   2. Publishers and publishing—Pennsylvania—Philadelphia—Biography. 3. Davis (F. A.) Company, Philadelphia. I. Marion, John Francis. II. Title.
Z473.C85A35   070.5'092'4 [B]   78-21182
ISBN 0-8036-2086-1

TO
ELIZABETH IRENE CRAVEN DAVIS
1874-1964

Aunt Irene,
   who kept it all together

CONTENTS

The present ownership and operation of the F.A. Davis Company can be traced to three events, each separated in time and occurring long ago—

—the founding of the company by F.A. Davis (1879)

—his marriage to my father's oldest sister (1895)

—my father's untimely death (1923)

BOBBY

My first business-related experience was meeting Aunt Irene. Unknown to me, she was determined that she would mold me into her kind of successor and one day I would take over the business.

On this same day I took my first long train ride. Irene's younger sister Ray had come to fetch me. She was mother to all the family orphans, a teller of tall tales and a sorceress who painlessly lured me away from my mother and brother. We left Newark for West Philadelphia to what is now the 30th Street Station then changed to a suburban train. The train windows were open and during the frequent stops I could hear firecrackers. It was the Fourth of July, 1927, just after my fifth birthday.

We arrived at Crum Lynne, where the New York to Washington line of the Pennsylvania Railroad passed over U.S. Route 13, known there as Chester Pike. As the train pulled out of the station Aunt Ray pointed across the tracks to the house, built in 1804, which was to be-

come my home for the next 20 years. The third floor room overlooking the tracks, and nearest to them, was mine.

When the family moved to Crum Lynne, the area was a summer resort for railroad executives. The Deshong Race Track was located behind the house. During World War I this was replaced by an assembly plant of the Baldwin Locomotive Works. The golf links on the other side of the Pike soon became dotted with jerry-built houses.

As we crossed the Pike I noticed that there were no sidewalks. The road had been widened, with room for only a narrow footpath between the curb and the steep bank to the house. We climbed stone steps to a screened-in porch which ran across the front of the house and along the side nearest the railroad. The windows and doors opened onto the porch. I quickly learned that no one used the front door or the parlor.

As we were walking along the side porch, a woman suddenly bolted out of the rear door, screaming and waving her arms wildly. I immediately turned and ran back to the screen door—my goal, the train platform. As soon as I was restrained I burst into tears and sobbed while Aunt Ray completed my introduction to Aunt Irene. It took more of Aunt Ray's magic to make me stay and even venture into the house. Aunt Irene liked to take care of her own clothes; so she had been ironing a few things when I arrived. She returned to her ironing, but I regarded her with suspicion and wouldn't go near the ironing board.

I was happy to find that they had a dog. However, I was not to touch the dog nor even go near her under any circumstances. The dog's name was Snap. During the next 11 years she put hundreds of teeth marks on my arms, legs, and face, but I still cried when the old bitch died. They also had cats which were relegated to the chicken house. Aunt Ray suggested we find them.

11

1912

Half of the side yard was a flower garden from the road to a wall which divided the property in half, front to back. Hollyhocks at the back of the garden shielded the chicken house from view of the train platform.

The chicken house was two stories with chickens roosting upstairs and down. The upper floor was divided into two rooms. One contained grain, mash, cracked oyster shell, fertilizer and an assortment of hand plows, spraying equipment and garden tools for cultivating the vegetable and fruit garden that took up the back of the property. That room I would return to for further investigation.

Besides the chickens there was a strange breed of animal called a guinea hen, producing brown speckled eggs with a strong or wild flavor. The hens traveled in a closely assembled flock and whenever approached would let out unearthly screeches in unison.

"Good watchdogs," Aunt Ray said.

"Why do we have Snap?" I asked.

A creek bordered the back of the property; so I was not surprised to see ducks and geese. There was an abundant supply of watercress where the cesspool overflowed into the creek. The moist soil at the bottom of the garden fed and nurtured the gigantic weeping willow, and once inside its branches I was shut off from the rest of the world. The obvious was to play Tarzan, but it could be a cave, a space ship, a submarine, a fort, or whatever I wanted it to be. Parting the branches and returning to the house through the corn and pole beans, both taller than I, made Aunt Ray's world of enchantment more fact than fantasy.

My tour delayed my meeting the other women in the house, Grandma Smith and Mrs. McCape. Two generations separated me from my aunts, three from Grandma Smith, and four from Mrs. McCape. They occupied the bedrooms at the back of the second floor.

Grandma Smith reminded me of a character

from a children's book, the one who scares little children. She always dressed in black. High-laced shoes showed beneath her ankle-length skirt. She wore a blouse and always a shawl over her shoulders, even on that hot July day. Her circulation must have been negligible since her face was only slightly grayer than her white hair, which was thin and collected in a bun on top of her head. Her skin was also thin and it seemed you could see through her scalp to her skull. Her face looked like a river bottom in a drought. I couldn't believe that anyone could have so many wrinkles. I never saw her laugh and her smile was like one an undertaker puts on a corpse.

I remember this stark figure sitting on the edge of her white counterpaned bed, the sun streaming in on her, reading her missal and holding a black wooden crucifix in her hand. She asked one day what I would do if I came home from school and found no one home, all the furniture gone, the curtains and shades removed, no rugs, and no wallpaper. I fled.

To keep busy she did her own laundry in the bathtub, using a small-sized washboard. She washed everything with a cake of Ivory soap: her clothes, her body, and her dentures. Once when she was bent over the washboard I asked her if I might wash my hands. She said it was all right and turned to me with her cake of Ivory. Somehow I dreaded touching that soap. She insisted. I took it and turned to the washstand. "In there," she said, pointing to the toilet, "we can't afford to waste water."

Grandma Smith and Mrs. McCape were mortal enemies. Whenever they saw each other they argued and screamed. Grandma Smith was the aggressor; so it was not surprising the Mrs. McCape kept her door closed. This suited everyone because we lived in fear that she would fall down the back steps. She walked with a cane and had to be helped down the stairs, ena-

14

bling her guide to close Grandma Smith's door before opening Mrs. McCape's.

Mrs. McCape was the last remnant of the F.A. Davis empire in Florida. The Pinellas Park Hotel was the last enterprise to go and Mrs. McCape was the last permanent resident. She had no family and no friends; so Aunt Irene brought her home to finish out her life. She received a small check each month which she dutifully endorsed over to Aunt Irene.

Mrs. McCape must have been a teacher, since it was decided that she should teach me to read. For a year she spent an hour a day with me, and I learned to read before I entered first grade. Only one other pupil in our class could read and we spent much of our time each leading half the class in reading circles. I was something of a hero, I was in love with our teacher, Miss Penny, and I was her pet. Instead of becoming a genius, my advanced status in the second and third grades led to boredom; in the fourth, to outright rebellion; and in the fifth, I was co-leader of a band of thieves. I was arrested, convicted, and reported to the chief of police once a month for a year.

Although Mrs. McCape and I spent all that time together, I never really learned anything about her. She was always that mysterious person behind the closed bedroom door—closed because of Grandma Smith, the back stairs, and a serious personal problem which was better confined to her room.

My room was mercifully shaded by a full-grown Oriental plane tree. The house had a tin roof, only a crawl space for an attic, and the bottom window sash was so large that the window could be raised only one fourth of the way. My iron bedstead was against the front window so that by raising my head I could see all four lanes of traffic and the double trolley tracks in the center of the highway. Without raising my head I could see both

15

train platforms, all four tracks, and the bridge. The abutments supporting the bridge were the cause of countless tragedies, most of which I was to witness.

By bedtime the trolleys were running about every half hour in each direction, the suburban trains about every hour. There was also an assortment of New York to Washington trains in bright red with the name Pennsylvania Railroad in gold letters. The through trains to the south had names like Atlantic Coast Line and Southern. Freight trains of 110 to 120 cars were a common sight.

There was a slight grade where we were, so the southbound trains went roaring by. A steam engine heading south with throttle open, and all its loose parts clanging and banging, would hit the open trestle and send me into the air parallel to the mattress as though by levitation. The northbound freights were fun because they had to slow down, sometimes to a stop, while an auxiliary engine from Baldwin was called into service to push them into Philadelphia. Only a railroad buff could thrill to the sounds of a stalled train, releasing air pressure, creaking, making the track click, and having couplings change grips. The real thrill came when the lead engine started and 120 couplings clanked and strained like the staccato of a machine gun, only to be picked up by the pusher engine ramming the couplings together again one by one back to the lead engine.

Traffic south could be frightening, traffic north was always exciting. It slowed to where I could read on the cars: "Fruit Grower's Express," "Burlington," "Illinois Central," and "Rock Island." It was difficult to realize that at the same time there was a constant flow of cars and trucks on U.S. Route 13 beneath the bridge.

I don't remember going to bed that first night, or going to sleep. At two a.m. I walked across the hall to Aunt Ray's room.

16

"Aunt Ray."
"What is it, Bobby?"
"Where is the telephone?"
"Why do you want the telephone?"
"I want to call my mother."

DAVIE

Frank Allston Davis (1850-1917) died five years before I was born and ten years before I arrived in Crum Lynne. There were no visible signs of his existence in the house, not even a portrait or a photograph. There was a sort of spiritual presence, though. The women in the family always referred to him as Davie and there was a change in the tone of their voices and a hesitation verging on reverence. He must have been a very kind and generous man.

F. A. Davis had spent his early years in the rugged farmland of Vermont where he attended normal school and became a teacher. However, his ambition and vision led him to Philadelphia for a career in business. At that time very few medical books were published in the United States. Most of them came from England, and William Wood & Company was the leading medical book publisher in the world. Mr. Davis became exclusive representative for them in Pennsylvania and

New Jersey. One day he called on Dr. John V. Shoemaker, Dean of the Medico-Chirurgical College (now the University of Pennsylvania Graduate School of Medicine) who had a manuscript he wanted published. Mr. Davis put it under his arm and thus in 1879 began the F. A. Davis Company. He was to develop a strong list of clinical books for his own company while continuing to sell for William Wood & Company. Contracts with salesmen dated 1880 named major works such as *The People's Cyclopedia of Universal Knowledge.*

History more or less repeated itself when I took over the company and signed an agreement to represent, in the United States, Blackwell Scientific Publications, Oxford, England. We have since developed the strongest publishing program in the company's history.

Aunt Irene married Davie in 1895. He had been a widower for seven or eight years with a son, Alonzo, 22 years of age and entering medical school. She was not yet 21. She had two teenage sisters, Kit and Ray, and a 5-year-old sister, Ann. Davie took them all in as his own family.

When my Grandfather Craven died the four girls were living with their Aunt Lizzie. She was a taskmaster of the Puritan ethic, upholding the rigid discipline of the Victorian era. Her strong Protestant persuasion was to deprive Aunt Ray of a love and a life of her own. What a joy it must have been for the four young ladies to escape to the old house on the other side of the railroad. Davie facetiously called it Tranquility Lodge.

The industrial zoning brought by Baldwin also brought a small steel mill to the other side of the old house. The house was sold when Davie died, and when I arrived on the scene it served as a warehouse for an automobile junk business.

The yard was cluttered with an assortment of wrecked and abandoned auto bodies. There were tires in the parlor, engines in the sitting room, transmissions

20

in the dining room, and upstairs one room contained radiators, another carburetors, and still another horns and accessories. I became a friend of the owner and was allowed to study the inventory when I wasn't in the way. In those days it was easy to know all the makes and models of cars. I knew them by their parts.

Aunt Irene never mentioned the old house. She acted as though it didn't exist and ignored my comments and inquiries about it. I was careful never to come home and announce that a "neat wreck" had just arrived and was at the front door awaiting disassembly.

If George Washington was noted as a general for his retreats, F.A. Davis was noted as an entrepreneur for his bankruptcies. Correspondence from the First National Bank of Clifton Heights, Pa., in 1880 indicates that the fledgling publishing company operated on notes issued to that bank. One of the bank's letters acknowledging a monthly payment delivers a strong rebuke for the previous month's payment not having been received. A cryptic P.S. asks: "What's he going to do next time?"

The F.A. Davis Company was declared bankrupt and the Receivers' Sale in 1900 was legal then but might be suspect today. F.A. Davis was one of three receivers named. Dr. John V. Shoemaker, the company's first author and at that time an officer of the company, bought the assets and returned them to Mr. Davis. The inventory for the sale printed by the company included all the bound stock, flat sheets, printing equipment, typesetting equipment (including each font), and such diverse items as one poker, one rake, one shovel, one ash can, one can for rags, one lye pot, and one horse, wagon and harness.

The bankruptcy led to the company's reincorporating in 1901. It would appear that at this time the company became a serious medical publisher. As editor Mr. Davis named Charles Euchariste de Medicis

21

Sajous, M.D., Sc.D., LL.D., a man of noble birth and advanced thinking in medicine. Mr. Davis showed himself a pioneer by acquiring the rights to *Studies in the Psychology of Sex* by Havelock Ellis. These rights were sold to Bennett Cerf of Random House in 1923 after Mrs. Davis declared, "This—the F.A. Davis Company—is not a sex house!"

Dr. Sajous developed the *Sajous Analytic Cyclopedia of Practical Medicine*, an eight volume reference source for practicing physicians. It became the major item for Davis salesmen. Sajous showed his advanced thinking in a book called *Internal Secretions and Principles of Medicine*. Published in 1903, it was a theoretical and not-too-scientific account of what today is called endocrinology. It was considered controversial but went through ten editions.

After reading the history of St. Petersburg, Florida, I wondered how F.A. Davis ever had the strength and ability to keep the publishing company going with all his activities in Florida. Let me capsulize that history. The land in Florida was bought by J.C. Williams, who persuaded Peter A. Demens to extend the Orange Belt Railway so the property could be developed as a city. As an enticement Demens, whose real name was Petrovitch A. Demenschoff, was given the right to name the city. He named it for his birthplace, Petrograd. Mr. Davis started advertising and promoting St. Petersburg, advancing its development years ahead of its time and ahead of all other Florida west coast cities.

The Florida connection started April 29, 1885, when Dr. W.C. Van Bibber at the annual convention of the American Medical Association in New Orleans read a paper entitled "A Contribution to Sanitary Science, relating especially to the climate and healthfulness of Pinellas Peninsula, Florida." Mr. Davis wanted to promote the area as a health resort and distributed reprints liberally

23

under the title, "The Healthiest Spot on Earth." He developed rheumatism and in 1889 went to Tarpon Springs, where he found immediate relief. He extended his publicity to *The Medical Bulletin* (The Cheapest and Best Medical Journal Published in the World for $1.00 per Year), published by the F.A. Davis Company. Later he started a magazine, *Florida*, printed by the company, and by 1906 distributed 10,000 copies of a booklet "Souvenir—St. Petersburg, the Pleasure City of the South" from the same printer.

Later in the winter of his first visit (1890) to Tarpon Springs, he met Jacob Disston, son of the founder of the saw manufacturing firm in Philadelphia. Interested in promoting Florida because his brother, Hamilton Disston, had just bought 4,000,000 acres from the state at 25 cents an acre, Jacob was to become the principal financier for the Davis enterprises. They started with an electric power plant, but the residents of Tarpon Springs weren't ready for it and remained loyal to their kerosene lamps. In 1897 the power plant was moved to the present site of St. Petersburg's Municipal Pier. From there expansion was planned east and west.

The existing pier was razed and a new one built 3,000 feet into the bay. This would allow ships to dock and increase trade with the Gulf, the Caribbean, and South America. They operated a steamship to Tampa, carrying passengers and freight from the railroad terminus there. The "electric pier" was the center of attraction for commerce and recreation. Anglers lined it and meeting ships became a social event.

To develop westward, a trolley line called St. Petersburg & Gulf Electric Railway Company was begun in 1904. It was cut through the palmetto groves to Boca Ciega Bay, where it was eventually met by a boat for Pass-a-Grille, the island which provided St. Petersburg with a beach on the Gulf. Not surprisingly, the trolley terminated in Disston City, now called Gulfport. Mr. Davis

24

persuaded George S. Gandy to lend financial aid and his expertise to the formation of the trolley company. Gandy was the man who put together the Philadelphia transportation system, which I remember as the Philadelphia Rapid Transit. We in Philadelphia think of our transportation system as always having been one unit. Actually it was a large group of small rail lines which Gandy brought together. Imagine traveling around the city today on the Frankford & Southwark Railroad Company, the Omnibus Company, the Holmesburg & Tacony Line, and the Doylestown & Willow Grove Line. Gandy later built a bridge across Tampa Bay (1923) and collected tolls until Franklin D. Roosevelt abolished them, declaring the bridge essential for our wartime needs. The development of the trolley line accompanied the extension, widening, and paving of Central Avenue. Land development companies moved in west of the city. F.A. Davis was there with the Florida West Coast Company.

Now to return to bankruptcies. In 1907 there was a localized money panic and the Davis empire collapsed. All the companies—land, railway, electric and ship—were thrown into receivership, severing all of Mr. Davis's relationship with St. Petersburg.

As soon as he gathered new resources, new associations, and made a huge acreage purchase northwest of St. Petersburg, F.A. Davis started a new town, Pinellas Park. The community was an agricultural one depending mainly on sugar cane. With the help of Hamilton Disston, Mr. Davis set up a cane syrup and sugar complex with a tram railway to carry the cane to the mill. The economy of the area was adversely affected by the beginning of World War I, and Pinellas Park was hit by two summers of heavy rains (including a hurricane) in 1915 and 1916. The downpour kept ahead of all the drainage projects.

"He was a visionary—he admitted it himself; in many ways he was impractical—his best friends said

25

PINELLAS PARK HOTEL

that about him. He foresaw progress, but he was years ahead of his time."[1] His demands on himself sent him constantly scrambling for working capital. As long as he was the cohesive force, it all kept going. Ten months after he died his Florida companies were bankrupt again.

Several observations about the electric company help place the Florida scene in perspective:

The Medical Bulletin, September 1897:

The latest improvement of magnitude in St. Petersburg is the completion and inauguration of the electric-light system. By this enterprise every part of the town is brilliantly illuminated. A formal inauguration of the new undertaking occurred in St. Petersburg on August 5 and was the occasion of much rejoicing among the inhabitants and invited guests. The trial illumination was a success in every particular. No pains had been spared by the company to provide the latest scientific devices, and the appliances connected with the work are of the most improved construction.

Benjamin F. Measy, Treasurer, F.A. Davis Company:

It certainly was the most primitive and out-of-date aggregation of machinery that had ever been collected, as it were, from the four corners of the earth, but after being put together under the able direction of A.P. Weller, manager of the company, the light it gave was certainly wonderful to behold.

History of St. Petersburg, by Karl H. Grismen, Tourist News Publishing Company, St. Petersburg, 1924:

27

The service given by the electric-light company was never above reproach during the early years of the company's existence. The equipment was inadequate and had a regrettable habit of breaking down at crucial moments. Such a breakdown occurred in August, 1904, while Mr. Davis was in the city with Wm. H. Houston and Frank Meazy, of Philadelphia, to whom he was extolling the merits of the plant. During their talk, both dynamos at the power plant went out of commission, plunging the city in darkness. This did not phase Mr. Davis, as he was used to even worse catastrophes. The records show that both Mr. Houston and Mr. Meazy continued to be identified with the company, so Mr. Davis must have drawn heavily upon his reserve store of eloquence. To the townspeople, Mr. Davis offered an apology for the breakdown and announced that the power company had secured new capital and would proceed immediately to get better equipment.

St. Petersburg Times:

After many patient years, we have all-night service at last. It is no longer necessary to leave off calling on your best girl at midnight for fear of the lights going out.

F.A. Davis was an American pioneer. Like most pioneers he neither benefited from his efforts nor received recognition in his lifetime. In 1923 the city of St. Petersburg honored him in a lavish ceremony. The *St. Petersburg Times* named him "Father of St. Petersburg." Today the F.A. Davis Company, at its one hundredth anniversary, still bears his name.

28

1. Much of the information in this chapter and all the quotes at the end are from *History of St. Petersburg* by Karl H. Grismen, Tourist News Publishing Company, St. Petersburg, 1924. Additional information came from *St. Petersburg and Its People* by Walter P. Fuller, Great Outdoors Publishing Company, St. Petersburg, 1972. I was reluctant to quote from this source because the author printed a letter I wrote him in 1964 (in its entirety). On the other hand, Mr. Fuller and his father were in business with F.A. Davis, and his book gives a more intimate account of what happened.

WALTER

Walter was off on July 4th when I arrived; so I didn't meet him until the next day. He was in the kitchen wearing a blue gingham apron and looking very much the butler. He greeted me warmly. Walter was tall, handsome, athletic, and strong, with the biggest smile I ever saw and a deep infectious laughter.

Suddenly I had someone to identify with in this old ladies' home. I followed Walter everywhere, even during his filthiest chores. In a Tom Sawyer type episode he taught me how to scrape and lime the chicken roosts. I must have annoyed him being at his heels all the time; but Walter was 27 and unmarried, and a little boy full of curiosity, worshiping him, must have brought him some pleasure.

I shared my hero with others. Walter batted in the clean-up spot on the local baseball team. On the day of a game we would finish our work early and I would watch Walter put on his uniform. It was a cream colored uniform with a blue and orange target on the back. The neatly sewed letters on the outside ring said Compton's Coal and Coke. He used strips of inner tubes for garters to hold up his pants and high socks. Walter would put on his street shoes and I would put his spikes in the basket on the handlebar of his bike and watch over them as he rode me to the game in Leiperville a mile away.

There was no fence around the field, the only seats were for the players and the backstop was less than adequate. Spectators stood or sat on the grass behind the players. There was a huge tree in left field, far enough out so that the left fielder could play his normal position just in front of it. Any ball that hit the tree on the fly was a ground rule double. That didn't bother Walter because if he hit to left the ball usually went over the tree. Center and right field were bounded by a dump of ashes and cinders from the local factories. Walter sent many an outfielder chasing across that dump only to return the ball to the infield long after he was safe at home. Walter had his own fans at all the games, among them a group of girls who squealed and giggled when he got up to bat, expressing their feelings about him in loud stage whispers. They screamed and jumped up and down when he hit the ball, while everyone else showed their approval with cheers and applause.

We used to do our shopping at an American Store (now Acme Markets) about a block beyond the baseball field. The gold on black lettered sign was a trademark on the bright yellow store. The nervous little manager would greet us personally since we always took away a large order. Walter would put me in the wagon and pull it to the store, but I'd have to walk home because the groceries filled the wagon. When the load got "too heavy" for him, he would let me push. There was an Italian store down the street from our regular grocery and the days we needed imported olive oil or grating cheese were special. I inspected the food hang-

32

ing from the ceiling and the bins of pasta and smelled the cheeses, herbs and other delicacies.

Leiperville was a mini melting pot of immigrants. Besides Italians I remember Lithuanians and Poles. The blacks clustered on a block of Holland Street on the other side of the Pike. Near Holland Street was the Leiperville Hotel. Baron Dougherty, the owner, was a boxing promoter and behind the hotel was a boxing arena where once a week in the summer there was a full card of boxing. Baron Dougherty's best-known property was a heavyweight named George Godfrey, who became a leading contender, but I'm not sure he ever got a shot at the title. It was here that Damon Runyon found most of his guys and dolls, not in New York as you might suspect. According to the old *Chester Times*, Runyon spent three months a year at the Leiperville Hotel gathering material in the bar and around the arena. It was in this arena that, as a kid, Bob Nilon sold his first bag of peanuts. From there he and his brothers Jack and Jim supplied factory workers with lunch from sandwich trucks, and today in Philadelphia Nilon Brothers caters the Veterans Stadium, the Army-Navy game, and hundreds of sporting events. Those early days must have influenced their interest in Sonny Liston.

The Baron lived up the hill from us and in the summer boxing rings were set up on his lawn. Another reward for finishing our chores early was to walk up the hill and watch the boxers sparring in the ring. I was denied access to the arena and the bar at the hotel, but I could sit on the edge of the ring with Walter and watch the boxers work out.

Our lives changed the next year when Aunt Irene bought Uncle Will's 1923 Jewett touring car. Mother had taken me to Aunt Lillian's farm in Virginia during the summer of 1928. Although Aunt Lillian was much older, they had an affinity as Craven in-laws. Since Uncle Will lived in Bristol, I was to return to Crum Lynne with him

33

when he delivered the Jewett. Uncle Will had a brand new Chevrolet Coupe with solid wheels right out of the Captain Easy comics. He was to drive the Chevy and his friend Hoover was to drive the Jewett and both would then return in the Chevy. Naturally I wanted to ride in the open car. Hoover was another teller of tall tales and soon had me spellbound just as Aunt Ray had done. At night I felt cold and was transferred to the warmth of Uncle Will's Chevy. I noticed the St. Christopher medal pinned to the upholstery above the windshield on the driver's side. When I asked him why the Jewett didn't have one he laughed and laughed. He knew what Aunt Irene would say, if it did.

Hoover was a strange man. He "shaved" by plucking at his meager beard with tweezers. He denied having a first name. I suspected that Hoover was an alias and that he had been in jail. He once worked for an electric company and in one bitter harangue after another swore vengence on all electric companies. When we arrived in Crum Lynne he told Aunt Ray that he could fix it so she would never have to pay for electricity again.

The electric meter was at the top of a long metal box and at the side was a knife switch to control current coming into the house. In the off position it gave access to a fuse box at the bottom. Hoover did something so the fuse box remained open when the current was on. He replaced the fuse with a plug and ran a cord to the nearest light in the ceiling, also replacing the bulb in the socket with a plug. Thus, the current flowed directly from the fuse box to the light fixture, by-passing the meter. It was alternating current in parallel so it could dead end at the end of the system and not have to return to the source. That rig was connected until about the 25th of each month. The fuse was replaced so that we would register the use of some electricity and after the meter was read on the first of the month Hoover's by-

34

pass was replaced. For all the years I can remember we had cheap electricity. Aunt Irene made a point of not understanding what was going on in the cellar.

I knew Walter could do anything, but if anyone had any doubts, the arrival of the Jewett proved it. The car was five years old and needed some work; for one thing, the rings were worn. Walter had never had an engine apart but with the aid of the owner's manual he drained the oil, dropped the pan, removed the crankshaft and then the pistons. He chiseled notches in each connecting rod so he would replace pistons in the same cylinders. Walter's best friend Buster helped and advised him that, "Those bearings is wore, too," so they were replaced. I wasn't allowed under the car but could lie on the garage floor and watch. As Walter busied himself, I inched my way under. I don't know how many times Walter took that engine apart, but he also operated on the transmission and the differential. He loved to work on the car because it took him away from all the menial tasks of the house, the garden and the chicken yard. He worked hard at tuning the engine, a delicate process with a manual spark and choke. He delighted in saying, "Give me your hand, Bobby," then applying the screwdriver to a spark plug, sending intermittant charges through my body. As long as he had a firm grip on each end of the charge, he didn't feel it. No matter how many times he did it I always fell for the trick. I was continually spellbound by Walter.

Eventually Walter cut the body off the old touring car and replaced it with a truck bed. We really needed a truck because the entire property was three acres and there were six tenant houses to keep in repair besides all the work required on our own house and by Aunt Ray's ambition in the garden. The summer I turned 12, Walter taught me how to drive the truck. When I was 14, Aunt Kit came up from Florida and wanted someone to drive her to Boston. Florida did not require a driver's

35

license and the qualifying age was 14. My first turn onto the open highway was behind the wheel of a brand new 1936 Oldsmobile.

Walter's biggest test came after one of Uncle Page's frequent visits. He had a friend in Washington, a Dr. Curtis, who had a 1914 Rolls Royce, also a touring car. The Rolls would not shift into second and third gear and Dr. Curtis said that anyone who could fix the transmission could have the car. It took Walter nine hours to drive from Washington to Crum Lynne in first gear. The transmission was repaired so fast that I don't even recall it. We were afraid to go anywhere in the Rolls, but it was the greatest joy ride ever, especially with the top down. There was no self starter and Walter was the only one around who could crank it. There was a small tank on the running board behind the tire well which had to be pumped up for fuel pressure. When the engine caught it had to be disengaged to let the fuel pump take over. The steering wheel had a throttle, spark, choke, and three other controls, six in all. I would sit behind the wheel while Walter cranked. As soon as the engine started I made several adjustments of the steering wheel controls as instructed and leaped to the far side of the car. Walter, meanwhile, would engage the fuel pump near the tank on the running board, then leap into the car behind the steering wheel. All the leaping was necessary because the British in their own way of thinking had not provided a door at the driver's seat. It was presumed that the car would always be driven by a chauffeur and cranked by a mechanic. The only time Walter ever swore at me was when my adjustments of the steering wheel controls failed and he had to crank the car again.

As I said, our lives changed with the arrival of the Jewett. No more bike rides, no more wagon rides, and not many long, long walks. Walter could think of more excuses to go to the feed store, the hardware store, the paint store, the grocery store, or even the gas

36

station because the car needed something. I was always sent with him to assure that he went directly to his destination and returned promptly. I was to report everything that happened. This naturally made Walter and me great conspirators. If Walter couldn't go, I couldn't go; besides, telling on Walter might spoil our relationship.

Whenever we went out, Walter headed straight for Holland Street. He would honk and Buster would come out and lean on the driver's side of the car. Buster had such a raspy, sandpaper voice that it was impossible for them to have a private conversation. I heard about all the things that happened at the last social. Gradually Walter's baseball fans they were talking about would come out and gather around Buster. One of them would grab Buster, sending him high in the air. Buster was very sensitive about that. Unnoticed, I shared their amusement. Sometimes Buster would go with us on an errand. When he did, I slid over to the middle of the seat and tried to interpret what they were saying. When Buster wasn't around one of the baseball fans would go with us. In that case I jumped in back so she could sit closer to Walter. I didn't mind because often when I realized who she was I got excited thinking about what Walter and Buster had planned for her after the next social.

Walter came from Floyd County where Aunt Lillian lived. His mother sent him north so he would have an opportunity that he could never have at home. If a dollar a day with room and board was that opportunity, then Walter had it made. His mother faithfully wrote to Aunt Irene; she in turn wrote back about Walter going to night school and how he made all the furniture in his room. He also made his own baseball bats which were so heavy that only he could bring them around fast enough to contact the ball. Aunt Irene kept account of his pay in a book much like a savings account. She doled out a dollar or two on a Saturday night depending on how convincing Walter was about his need. Aunt

38

Irene used his mother's latest letter to convince him of her own personal concern for him and to explain her own frugality.

One day I was told that Walter was very ill and that I was not to go near his room. Dr. Nelson was coming to see him; so I knew that if the family doctor was called it had to be serious. No one would tell me what was wrong. I was so worried and upset at not seeing him that I nagged Aunt Ray until she finally told me. Walter had syphillis. "He couldn't find a decent, refined, religious girl to go with, he had to cohabit with those sluts who cohabit with other men."

My idol had fallen. Walter told me later that the worst part of having syphillis was the nausea that came after taking those ugly green liquid capsules. The only thing worse than those capsules was Aunt Ray or Aunt Irene moralizing about Walter's choice of friends, "and I don't want to see that Buster around here again!"

I had to struggle with the idea that Walter was involved with sin. What really bothered me was being deprived of his company while he was ill. I thought he deserved better from his fans.

Finally, Walter found a decent, refined, religious girl. He married the parson's daughter. It meant that he would leave and I would be very much alone. A very dramatic event filled my days, and nights, softening the blow. The railroad and the highway department tore down the old bridge and built a new one. They could only do one track at a time and they had to work at night. For two years I watched an assortment of cranes, work trains, and more equipment than Lionel could ever dream of, right outside my window.

The old bridge had two six-foot wide granite abutments that divided the highway into three double lanes. When the trolley cars ran in the middle section, the abutments were problem enough for the cars in the outside lanes. When buses were substituted for the trol-

39

leys, the center lanes were paved so the motorist had a shot at two outside lanes or one inside lane. Whenever I went to bed on a foggy night, I knew I would be wakened by the sound of a crash. Usually the car or cars involved were still in motion when I jumped up. My reflexes were conditioned to the noises around that bridge. Some cars plowed straight ahead, some veered off the abutment and crashed into the wall, some rolled over, some burned. In eight years, 26 people were killed and injury-inflicting accidents occurred on the average of once a month.

I wasn't allowed beyond the front porch when there were day-time accidents. If the weather was good most accidents occurred at dinner time. Walter would fly out of the kitchen and be first on the scene. He got $7.50 a day as a witness and while he had to bargain with Aunt Irene over the money he also got out of work the days he testified. One night there was a large crowd in the middle of the street looking over a minor accident (internal injuries only) when a drunk came through the middle in the opposite direction and bowled over 13 people. When Walter got through helping to haul bodies to the hospital that night, his beautiful brown skin looked ashen purple.

So the Pennsylvania Railroad and the State Highway Department built a monument to Walter. I never looked at the new bridge without thinking of him. Walter was the man in my life when I needed one so badly.

LONNIE

J.C. Allred was sales manager when I joined the company. He was a handsome man with platinum hair and a honey-dripping North Carolina accent that belied his fierce temper. One day Harry, the treasurer, held up a salesman's commission check. J.C. went to Harry's desk, picked him up out of his chair, held him up by the armpits and said, "Are you going to send out that check or am I going to throw you down the stairs?" J.C. was a big decision maker in the company and decisions such as these led to an early coronary.

J.C. once told me that F.A. Davis was the "finest salesman I ever met in my life." He freely admitted that everything he owned in this world he owed to F.A. Davis. F.A. took him out on the road in 1905 and showed him the ropes. J.C. was the first salesman to own a car (in 1909) and worked Indiana because Indiana had the first highways, unpaved but laid in crushed stone. He said that he drove for hours without seeing another car and

43

when a cloud of dust appeared on the horizon he would prepare to stop. Any exchange with another person, usually another salesman, was welcome. They would admire each other's car, sometimes enough to make a deal. All it took was the exchange of license plates and a few dollars one way or the other. "Horse trading" was in their blood.

He was only 65 when I arrived—I say *only* because that was the average age of management. Nevertheless, he was guarding his health and wanted very much to retire. Aunt Irene desperately held on to him until I could learn more about his job, because an interim sales manager just didn't suit her plans. They worked out a compromise whereby J.C. would spend winters in Florida and summers in Cape May. I was made Assistant Sales Manager to run the sales office and oversee the activities of 25 hard-bitten commission salesmen.

No one told me what to do and no one showed me how to sell our big item, the 15 volume *Cyclopedia of Medicine, Surgery, Specialties*. So I decided to learn from experts and applied for a part-time job with *Encyclopedia Americana*, evenings and Saturday. I was interviewed by their sales manager, took home the sales kit, memorized the sales talk, came back and regurgitated it to his satisfaction. He arranged for me to go out with a trainer the next day.

"Before you go I'd like you to meet our District Vice President, Mr. Alley."

I had heard about Alley from our advertising manager and knew that he was a big man in the book trade. He looked over my application and then looked up.

"F.A. Davis. Let me see, did you ever know a Doc Davis?"

I was delighted that this big man in publishing knew something about our company.

"He was F.A. Davis's son, Alonzo. He's dead now but I've met him. Why do you ask?"

"He was the best goddamned pool shot I ever met in my life!"

Alonzo B. Davis (1873-1942) was tall, slender, wore a waxed moustache and goatee, carried a silver headed cane, had his coat trimmed in fur, and for a time drove a Stutz Bearcat. He studied medicine and in his senior year his father was called into the dean's office. Alonzo was not to graduate. I don't know what went on behind that closed door, but Alonzo got his M.D. He never took the licensure exam to practice.

Aunt Irene said that his mother died when he was about 14 and his father "spoiled him rotten" in his efforts to make up for his loss. He worked for the company for a time, but publishing in medicine stimulated him no more than medicine itself. Therefore, his father sent him to Florida to look after his interests there. Alonzo was very excited about land speculation, showed his father's prowess as a salesman, and flourished. In addition to his father's interests, Alonzo made good on some of his own speculations.

After F.A. Davis died in 1917, Aunt Irene suspected that there was a conspiracy and that Alonzo had lined up with the other principals in the Florida companies, forcing them into bankruptcy. The same principals bought the companies back for virtually nothing. This struck a severe blow to the estate and led Aunt Irene's attorney to advise her to give up Florida and devote her full time and attention to the only thing of real value, the publishing company.

At one point the situation was so serious that she had to come up with $10,000 or lose control of the company. She went to the Delaware County Trust Company in Chester and saw a man who called himself Colonel Campbell. She told him her story and concluded it by saying that she had no collateral and wasn't sure how she could pay it back. "All we need is your word, Mrs. Davis." We never went to Chester for shopping or any other reason without paying the Colonel a visit.

At this same time, Alonzo was living in a $100,000 house in the fashionable Overbrook section of Philadelphia. He was a fancy dresser, liked sports cars, and high living. This made Aunt Irene's struggle all the more bitter. Even though Aunt Irene was younger than Alonzo and certainly never filled the role of mother to him, she always spoke of him more with compassion than distaste.

After I took over the production department, a photoengraving salesman took me to lunch. He said, "I think I know you well enough now to tell you how I got the Davis account. Of course, I wouldn't want any of this repeated to Mrs. Davis, okay?"

"Sure."

"My wife had a friend who lived in a nice apartment but didn't work and didn't seem to have any means of support. My wife and this girl were pretty close friends and finally she told my wife that someone was keeping her. They were limited as to the places they could go because this guy was married, and so my wife invited them over for dinner one night. I knew the girl, of course, and she introduced her boyfriend as Lonnie—Alonzo B. Davis, all the girls called him Lonnie. Anyway, he saw to it that I got the Davis account, and I've remained silent until now."

When the crash came and the Florida land boom was over, Alonzo had nothing. Aunt Irene persevered and had the F.A. Davis Company well under her control. I don't know what contact they had after that, but when I met Alonzo he was suffering from diabetes which eventually resulted in gangrene.

Walter's successor lasted only a year. Aunt

46

Irene had bought a 1936 Chevrolet and now she was without a driver. I was only 15 but necessity forced her to swear I was 16. I was back on the road again.

One of our duties was to pay regular visits to Alonzo because he was ill. I dreaded them because of the awful sickroom smell. Finally I caught on that Aunt Irene was slipping a check to Alonzo's wife, Tillie, whenever we visited. She gave them $50 a week all through his illness and God knows how much she paid in medical bills.

It never occurred to Aunt Irene that a son of F.A. Davis would die in need.

JUST A POOR LITTLE WIDOW

Ken Bussy, a former colleague and now Executive Editor with Lea and Febiger said Aunt Irene "was, in her later years, a tiny, energetic lady dressed in the fashion of another day to be seen resolutely commuting to the office on the Pennsylvania Railroad. Her sweetness and gentility cloaked a strong will and an ability to manipulate people to her advantage."[2]

Ed Irvine had become treasurer in the wake of a purge by the George S. May Company, business consultants. Ed had worked for some of the Robert C. Young companies in New York, commuting for 17 years, so locating in Philadelphia meant more time at home. He had an attractive, dedicated, and always pleasant wife. His seven children, all good looking, were the nicest I

2. R. Kenneth Bussy: *Philadelphia's Publishers and Printers; An Informal History.* Philadelphia Book Clinic, 1976.

49

ever met. Ed felt that his big corporation experience would not only help us financially but also bring sound management principles to our small, loosely-run company.

After two months he felt confident of his acceptance: he was respected and solidly a part of the decision-making process in the company. None of this meant much, however, unless he had the approbation of the President, Mrs. Davis. He was beginning to feel comfortable with her when one day after lunch she called him in.

Aunt Irene's office had a circle of heavy leather upholstered chairs ready for an instant meeting. In fact, her office was the only conference room in the building. The visitor's seat was one of those chairs nearest the door facing the windows. I understand that some people put their visitors facing the windows to put them at a disadvantage.

"Mr. Irvine, we don't seem to have the caliber of men around here that we used to have."

Ed wondered why she hired him.

"Now take George B. Johnson, for example. He would go out and meet our authors. He called on our dealers all over the country. Many's the time he would call on a dealer and collect his account—bring the money home with him. If we had editorial problems George B. would get at the heart of the matter and solve the problem. I remember him sitting there. . . ."

Ed ate very heavy lunches and now the room was getting warm, the sun was streaming in the windows, the objects in the room were becoming indistinct. As Aunt Irene talked, Ed saw the form of George B. Johnson in that chair. She continued weaving her spell and Dr. Sajous joined Mr. Johnson, then Benjamin Measy, the original treasurer, became part of the meeting, C. T. Crandall, sales manager, was next, and even

50

Van Horn who ran the printing plant became part of the array.

Ed came to me afterward, shaken. "She's another Sarah Bernhardt! What do you suppose it meant?"

I had to laugh. It was all too familiar.

"It meant, don't get too big for your britches, Ed. Let me tell you a story. When we were in the hands of the bank in 1933 they sent their man to sit on our Board. He became, in effect, the general manager. When we were clear of debt in 1938, we still had our line of credit with the same bank and it was agreed that the bank's man would stay on as a consultant. After the war he went to Aunt Irene and explained that he had been with the company over 12 years, he liked the business, and was confident that it had a good future. The bank was a large company, he had gone about as far as he could go there, and he would like to work for a company that he felt he was really a part of. He offered to buy some stock of the company and give it his full time. She replied simply, 'That's interesting, Mr. Jackson, let's give it some thought.' A year passed and nothing was mentioned. Finally Jackson went to Aunt Irene and said, 'Mrs. Davis, a year ago I offered to buy some stock of the company.' She said, 'Yes, I've been meaning to discuss that with you.'"

I've heard Aunt Irene's version of that meeting, but my point for Ed was the result. The editor who sat at the foot of the stairs had become a close friend of Jackson. He told me that he looked up from his desk and saw an old man struggling down the stairs. When he looked again he realized that it was Jackson and ran to assist him. He was pale, moist, and trembling. The editor administered to him for over an hour.

"What happened?" he asked.

Aunt Irene had told him, in terms he could understand, what she thought of men who tried to take advantage of her . . . just a poor little widow.

52

When I finished college the going rate for graduates without any special skills was $50 a week. I was determined to work for another company for at least two years and then join the Davis Company. No matter what argument I offered Aunt Irene for working somewhere else, she was determined that I was going to start with Davis. It offered me more opportunities: an entree to so many places, a chance to travel that no other job could provide. She would not take no for an answer. After I graduated, I wanted the summer off. I got the summer off and she agreed to match the going rate.

One of the troubles with nepotism is that unrelated emotions influence sound business decisions. In February of my senior year I announced my intention of marrying. Aunt Irene was not about to approve any marriage unless she could select the bride, the time, and the place. She didn't confront me with her disapproval, but several days later she came up with a startling piece of information. In this postwar, poststrike car shortage she had found someone who could get us a new Chrysler. I could drive and we could do all the things we had done before the war when we had a car. We could take trips together, we could visit the family, we could shop, we could do with ease all the things that were now so difficult. We could also keep Bobby at home and get this silly notion of marriage out of his head.

Aunt Irene bought the car. I must admit I was thrilled, and the family was drawn closer together. Nevertheless, I still had a lust to leave. Martie insisted that I graduate before we set a date and she would not go "steady" until the date was set. Her wisdom created a relationship that was always true and feelings that ran very deep. Finally accepting my determination to marry, Aunt Irene helped me to resolve the religious differences, resolved in a way that was never questioned by my in-laws and made our association a warm and wonderful family experience.

53

We were to be married in New Hope, Pennsylvania, by a Justice of the Peace, a certain Donald E. Delacey. Dressed in a white suit, I descended the stairs from the third floor, ignoring the fourth-from-the-bottom-step and the two floor boards that squeaked. I entered Aunt Irene's room to say good-bye—not good-bye for now, but GOOD-BYE.

"I guess you're ready."

"Yes."

"Where is it you're getting married?"

"New Hope."

"That's interesting. How are you getting there?"

"I'm taking the car."

"I haven't made any arrangements for you to take the car."

"You mean you won't let me have the car on my wedding day?"

"No, you're to leave the car here, in the garage."

"Well, I'm taking the car. Call the State Police if you like. You've got the license number and they should find us easily."

The police never came after us. We returned three days later, left the car, and took off for California on one of the first "non-stop" DC-6 flights, only because an unexpected check from Aunt Kit's estate arrived providing us with a honeymoon we never dreamed could happen.

We returned penniless, condemned to a fourth floor walk-up, ready once again to face the hard facts of life. Naturally, the first thing that happened when we left was that Aunt Irene sold the car—at a profit. Cars were still hard to come by. I reported for work wondering how I was going to make it until payday.

"Well, how was your trip?"

"Oh, it was wonderful! And here I am ready to go to work."

"I've been talking to Harry. We have a lot of em-

54

ployees who have been here for years. None of them make anywhere near $50 a week. They just wouldn't understand if I brought in my nephew—just a boy, with no experience—and paid him more than they were getting, after all these years."

"But you promised me $50 a week."

"We can only pay you $40 a week to start."

I have always said that as long as people act in character I can handle anyone or any situation. It's when they step out of character that I worry. Aunt Irene's usual method of handling a new situation was to discuss it with everyone she encountered, even the conductor on the train, get their ideas, pick their brains, and then go into a long thought process before making a decision. Not so with the George S. May Company. When she told me about them, they were coming, and I was the first person she told. Something was up.

What it really amounted to was that Aunt Irene realized that certain people in the organization had to go and she couldn't wield the ax. When the May people got to Harry, they told me that he had done everything possible to undermine me and raise doubts about my credibility with my aunt. He had a knife in my back all the time and whenever he saw Aunt Irene he gave it a new twist. They cited examples.

"How do you feel about that?" asked the project engineer.

"I feel sorry for the guy," I said.

"You feel sorry for the guy! After all we just told you?"

"Yeah, he's not very bright. He could raise all the doubts he wanted but I'd have to destroy myself to get fired. He should have lined up with me, not against me."

"You feel sorry for the guy." He turned to his companion. "Did you ever hear anything like that? Did you?"

55

He never did.

It was interesting to watch the May Company at work. First they sent in a man to do a preliminary survey; he was followed by a man who would make recommendations, really the salesman; and he was backed up by two accounting types who remained on through the entire project. They were always either interviewing, in conference, or on the phone to headquarters. They always stayed after hours and called in. It was as though they had a direct line to George S. May himself.

At the end of the second day the salesman poked his head in my office.

"Where do you eat dinner around here?"

"The Cheshire Cheese in the Sheraton is the newest place. It's good if you can stand the service and your waiter doesn't dump the salad in your lap."

"How about having dinner with me there?"

"Well, yeah. I have to call home first."

We ordered drinks but before we took the first sip he got right down to business.

"Usually we are retained by the President of the company and sometimes we have trouble because there is a power struggle among the executives. In this case we have been retained by the owner. We don't expect any trouble from any of the employees, they'll do whatever we tell them. There's only one person who can cause us any trouble."

"Who's that?" I asked, thinking of Harry.

"You."

"Me! Why me?"

"Because you're family. You're the only one who can throw a monkey wrench in the works. What do you say, are you with us or against us?"

"Well, it never occurred to me not to cooperate. I assume you're going to act in the best interests of the company."

56

"Good. You know your aunt loves you very much. Oh, she'll never throw her arms around you and *tell* you she loves you. She's a person who can't express her emotions. Just in two days, talking to her, I know that she wants the Davis Company to keep going more than anything else in the world. You're the one person who can make that happen. She wants you to have it. Just think! One day this will all be yours.

"I want you to do me a favor. Stop fighting with your aunt."

"I don't fight with my aunt!"

"Yes, you do. You object to everything she wants done and you scream your head off when she won't let you have your way. Don't fight her. Don't let the everyday crap ruin your future. Just think one thing: 'One day this will all be mine.' It makes the everyday crap look stupid, doesn't it?"

"Yeah, I guess so."

"Now promise me you won't fight with your aunt, that you'll agree with everything she says, no matter what, and don't get upset when she won't let you do what you want. You'll be the happiest man alive. Do it now, while you still have a chance. I'll tell you what. I'll guarantee that if you do what I just asked for three months, you and your aunt will be the closest of friends for the rest of your lives."

He was wrong.

It only took one month.

ROYALTY

To me, Dr. Sajous was a paradox. He was born in 1852 of French parents on a ship returning from America as it neared the French coast. The ship must have had both power and sail since only seven years earlier the first propeller driven ship crossed the Atlantic. He was the son of Count Charles Roustan de Medicis-Jogoigne, head of a prominent Florentine family of French-Flemish origin, and Marie Pierette Cort. Although he was born of royalty, he lived most of his life in the United States. Dr. Sajous was educated privately in France but received his medical education at the University of California and Jefferson Medical College. He studied endocrinology in Europe and introduced the subject to the United States; held the first chair in endocrinology in the history of medicine but did not make a single original contribution to endocrinology; and was the first president of The Endocrine Society but is not remembered today as the pioneer in medicine who was honored on two continents for his work. Even having a name like Charles Euchariste de Medicis and taking the name of his stepfather, Sajous, is paradoxical.

After graduating in medicine, Dr. Sajous specialized in laryngology. He became the first Lecturer in Laryngology at Jefferson and later Dean and Professor of Laryngology at Medico-Chirurgical College. It was at the College that he and F.A. Davis became acquainted since Dr. Sajous succeeded Dr. John V. Shoemaker as Dean and wrote two manuals for the company, *Lectures on the Diseases of the Nose and Throat* and *The Treatment of Hay Fever.* He was Professor of Therapeutics at Temple University Medical School and later Professor of Applied Endocrinology (the first in history) at the University of Pennsylvania Graduate School of Medicine, a post which he held until his death in 1929.

In 1888 he began to digest medical articles as editor-in-chief of the *Annals of the Universal Medical Sciences.* Five volumes a year were published until 1896, 45 volumes altogether, and a total of 500,000 volumes were sold in nine years. Publication discontinued in the Panic of 1896, the year that the F.A. Davis Company announced its bankruptcy. After the turn of the century when the company was reorganized Sajous went on to edit his *Analytic Cyclopedia of Practical Medicine* for general practitioners. Published in eight volumes; in time over 240,000 volumes were sold.

Medical Life said:[3]

Dr. Sajous was called "the most robbed man in America"—many writers, unwittingly or otherwise, claim endocrinological offspring whose real parentage will be found in the 1st edition of *The Internal Secretions and Principles of Medicine.*

3. *Medical Life* Vol. 25, p. 16, 1925.

60

Although he has stood apart from the main trend of American medicine, he is one of our few physicians with a therapeutic message; and in his own lifetime he has seen himself become an historic figure, and he must realize that the influence of Sajous will be felt by coming generations of medical men.

The paradox persists. Professor Ernst Knobil, President of The Endocrine Society, addressing the Fifty-Ninth Annual Meeting said,[4]

In 1892, Sajous dropped his practice and institutional appointments in Philadelphia and returned to France for a period of study with none other than Brown-Séquard. Nine years later, he published the work entitled, *The Internal Secretions and Principles of Medicine* in two volumes and 1,873 pages, which went through nine editions, the last in 1922. For these grandiose labors he received more honors than one can easily recount. Dr. Sajous was with little question one of the leading figures in the medicine of his time.

His obituary in *American Medicine* began with the statement that "The name of Dr. Charles E. de M. Sajous will go down to posterity as one of those pioneers to whom medicine owes each forward stride it makes." Clearly this was not to be. Unhappily, our first president, so eminent in his own day, not so many years ago, and despite his prodigiously voluminous writings on the subject, cannot be remembered for a single original contribution to En-

4. *Endocrinology* 101:5, 1977. I am indebted to Professor Knobil for sending a copy of his speech to me before publication and allowing me to quote from it.

61

docrinology. The reason for this sad conclusion is simple: he was blind to the ways of science. He even chose to engage it in mortal combat, a battle which he was bound to lose.

He goes on to resolve the debate with scientific data beyond the scope of this history and its author. Nonetheless, Dr. Sajous was a remarkable man. Another pioneer, he led the way for others without knowing the ultimate destination.

NOBILITY

The socially prominent families of Philadelphia settled along the main line of the Pennsylvania Railroad giving new meaning to that old railroading term. Aunt Irene aspired to be part of that society, which her Aunt Lizzie instilled in her, but living on a secondary route of the railroad was impetus enough. She entertained extensively for and with her husband, and renouncing her social life after his death was one of the greatest sacrifices she was to make.

In any conversation Aunt Irene invariably brought up the name of an eminent person she had met or wished she had. I thought she was the world's worst name dropper. Looking back I realize that she was reliving a part of her life which she cherished and, of course, which I had not shared.

Her link with the social world was John Joseph McElroy, Jr., Vice President and Manager, Textbook Department. He signed his name "J.J." and insisted on being called Jack at first meeting. Although Jack and Aunt Irene were very close they were uncomfortable on a first name basis. He called her "Boss Lady" and she called him "MisterMcElroydear." Jack's blonde wife, Florence, was attractive, charming, able, and efficient. They entertained constantly and were entertained in return and were part of many important social events. Jack spent hours regaling Aunt Irene with stories about people he and Florence met and affairs they attended. She listened to their plans for new parties as though she were a part of them. I'm sure she fantasized about being hostess once again.

It isn't surprising, therefore, that in 1954 Jack and Florence gave a party for the company's 75th Anniversary. It was carefully planned for May when the azaleas were in bloom. I remember it as a warm day, more like summer than late spring. The McElroys did a remarkable job of entertaining all the employees of the company and those closely associated with it.

The singular event that lingers in my mind was the arrival of George Morris Piersol, M.D. (1880-1966). Dr. and Mrs. Piersol knew the McElroys socially so there was a warm and extended greeting at the door. Mrs. Piersol was an elegant woman with the bearing and manner of refinement ingrained for several generations. He was both charitable and benevolent, spoke softly, and was perhaps the finest gentleman I have ever met.

Aunt Irene greeted the Piersols with her usual histrionic flair and then Dr. Piersol made sure that Mrs. Piersol was comfortably seated. Before he would seat himself, he shook hands with everyone at the party. Clerk or janitor, it mattered not. Dr. Piersol took an interest in everyone. Even though he usually came to the office only twice a week, he seemed always to know something about each one he saw, an ailment, a vacation, where the children were in school—always something.

66

Aunt Irene took great pride in her association with Dr. Piersol. She loved to tell people that his middle name was a family name that came from Robert Morris, who helped finance the American Revolution. He did use his middle name, signing in the old-fashioned way, Geo. Morris Piersol. His close friends called him "Morrie." I was awed by Dr. Piersol but never uncomfortable with him. He was too warm and good humored for that. He even had time for a little joke with the boys in the warehouse on his way to and from the parking lot.

His achievements were abundant and varied. He received his B.S. and M.D. from the University of Pennsylvania. At the Hospital of the University he was intern, resident, and chief resident. At the Medical School he was Instructor, Associate, Professor of Clinical Medicine, and Professor of Physical Medicine and Rehabilitation. He was director of a center for instruction and research in the latter field and the center was named for him in his lifetime. At the Graduate School of Medicine he was Professor of Medicine and served as Dean (1954-1957). His father, George A. Piersol, was Professor of Anatomy before him and author of a popular book on the subject.

Both his father's parents were physicians; his grandmother was one of the first graduates of Woman's Medical College (now The Medical College of Pennsylvania). Dr. Piersol served as Professor of Medicine at the Woman's Medical College; was associated with five area hospitals, the Veterans Administration, and the U.S. Army; and was Medical Director of the Bell Telephone Company for 25 years. He belonged to many medical organizations but the most important was the American College of Physicians. He was the third person named Master of Medicine by the College and served as President, Treasurer, Secretary-General (20 years), and Chairman of the Credentials Committee for many years. He wrote the College history *Gateway of Honor* (1962).

"Dr. Piersol's training was primarily along clinical lines and he antedated current enthusiasm and facilities for research, recognizing the impact that scientific developments were having on the fundamental aspects of clinical problems. He brought new knowledge to the attention of the profession recognizing the necessity of organizational approaches to the solutions of medical problems. He played an important role in the emergence of internal medicine as a specialty."[5]

Dr. Piersol was associated with at least four medical journals but his work as Editor of the *American Journal of the Medical Sciences* from 1911 to 1922 attracted the Davis Company to him. "It was his constant endeavor to keep the Journal on a high plane, as regards both the literary and scientific quality of its pages, and that he achieved success is evidenced by the high esteem in which the Journal is held by the profession throughout the civilized world . . . under Dr. Piersol's editorship the writings of the foremost men in all branches of medical science have appeared in its pages . . ."[6]

And so it was that after Dr. Sajous's death Dr. Piersol took on the monumental task of editing *The Cyclopedia of Medicine, Surgery, Specialties.* As the title implies the scope of the work increased and so did the size—from 8 to 15 volumes. There were over 900 monographs, and during the next 33 years thousands of authors contributed material to keep the monographs up to date and to provide an annual supplement of advances in medicine.

5. *Transactions and Studies of the College of Physicians of Philadelphia,* Fourth Series, Volume 34, 1966-67. Memoir of George Morris Piersol, M.D. (1880-1966).
6. *American Journal of the Medical Sciences,* New Series 163, January-June, 1922, p. ix.

Dr. Piersol relied on an able Associate Editor to keep contact with the many people involved in the publication of the *Cyclopedia*. Edward L. Bortz, M.D. (1895-1970) had a charm of his own, the kind that helped elect him President of the American Medical Association for 1947-1948. Dr. Bortz graduated from Harvard University and its medical school. He did graduate work at the Mayo Clinic and the Universities of Vienna, Berlin, and Illinois. He was a pilot in the Army Air Corps during World War I and a captain in the Medical Corps of the Navy during World War II. The Navy remembers him best for his duty at Iwo Jima with the Marines and at Nagasaki. I remember him for intervening when my imperious commanding officer insisted that I return from home to active duty while suffering from pneumonia with a fever of more than 100 degrees. Actually the C.O. wanted to put me in the Naval Hospital in Philadelphia. Dr. Bortz was then C.O. of the Hospital and refused to take me. As Aunt Irene put it to *my* C.O., "You're the people who made him sick. You don't think we're going to put him back in your hands until he's well, do you?" I finally returned to duty with great trepidation only to be treated with a respect I had not known before.

When I started attending the Annual Meeting of the American College of Physicians, the college arranged a concert by the symphony orchestra of the host city on Monday evening of the meeting. When the college meeting convened in Philadelphia in 1955, Dr. Bortz was on the Board of Governors and did his best to entertain the members. They toured the new Lankenau Hospital of which he was very proud. He served on the staff there for 44 years and was head of one of the two medical services for 30 of those years. He invited the Board of Governors to a black tie dinner at the Union League on the night of the concert by the Philadelphia Orchestra. Dr. Bortz was a member of the Philadelphia Orchestra Association; so I assume it was no coincidence

69

that the concert was held up until Dr. Bortz's party was seated in the boxes on the right of the Academy of Music. The full house quieted when Eugene Ormandy came to center stage, bowed to Dr. Bortz and the Board of Governors, the audience in general, and then turned and raised his baton. Dr. Bortz and Dr. Piersol each had his own way of making one feel important in his presence.

AN AMERICAN ORIGINAL

I was eight- or nine-years-old when I first visited the company. The printing presses and typesetting machines were still there. Due to operating losses in 1931 they were sold and the printing plant became a warehouse. It would be up to two men, both new to the scene, to fill that warehouse: Dr. Piersol and a man named Taber.

On that first visit I met the night watchman, Charlie, and inspected his unloaded revolver. In the daytime he operated an auto repair shop next door and on subsequent visits I would look in on him. The women in the office would usually make a fuss over me.

Because they knew me as a boy, everyone in the office called me Bobby. That is, until I became President. I was then Mr. Craven except to a few of the older employees, close to Aunt Irene, who respectfully referred to me in private as Bob. All but one man, Mr. Taber never called me anything but Bobby and he lived eight years after I became President.

Mr. Taber had a right to call me Bobby or anything else he wanted. He had lived a lifetime before he came with the company and he was 52 years older than I. He had been a farm hand, janitor, bookkeeper, cashier, catalog editor, magazine editor, book review editor, educational representative, and general manager and editor for school books before I was born! He had also published an anatomical chart and a dictionary for nurses.

Clarence Wilbur Taber was born in Jersey City in 1870. Four years later, after his father died, the family moved to Newark, New Jersey. They remained there until 1884, a year after his mother remarried. His stepfather moved them to the Dakota Territory not far from present-day Pierre, South Dakota.

Mr. Taber described the stark realities of the prairies in his books and manuscripts. He made constant reference to the fact that there was "not a tree in sight."[7] He told of the proximity of the Indians and the buffalo bones left by the indiscriminate shooting of animals by white hunters. There was no fuel. Coal was hauled by wagon from the nearest depot 50 miles away. Buffalo chips were a necessary substitute for firewood. The streams were usually dry and because there was little water, wells had to be dug deep. Prairie fires were a constant menace and temperatures ranged from 40 below zero to 120 degrees above. Mr. Taber walked three and a half miles to school. Children today, whose cars fill the high school parking lots, should note that he was not permitted to ride one of the family horses to school even though the boys at school built a sod barn for horses.

7. *Autobiography of Clarence Wilbur Taber* (unpublished). Mr. Taber's daughter, Mrs. Mildred Taber Clark, kindly sent me this autobiography written for the family. All quotes, except as noted, and much of the detailed information is from this autobiography. I am grateful to Mrs. Clark for her generous help.

74

His stepfather built a house that "was only a board structure covered by tar paper and building paper on the inside. In the winter the snow would blow through the nail holes and awaking in the morning I would find my breath frozen to the buffalo robe that covered me, and a pile of snow on the floor." Life at home was made unbearable by the stepfather, a heavy-drinking tyrant driven to frequent rampages and ranting that shook the walls of the house. At 17, Mr. Taber ran away from home, following the path of an older brother and a stepbrother. After three days of tramping through the snow, wind and rain, he landed at a farm which had made known its need for a "hand."

Later his brother wrote him that he could make more on a threshing crew; so he joined his brother. His brother and one of his school teachers helped him build a 10 x 10 sod house, near his own home, to live in during the winter. The following season he worked a claim for the woman who ran the hotel in town and while working the corn crop he suffered from sunstroke. She got him a job as a stableman and janitor to the local banker. His salary was paid directly to the hotel for his room and board. To earn pocket money he did odd jobs, such as packing dirt (actually manure) around houses for the winter. When the banker was out of town Mr. Taber was watchman, staying in the banker's room in the back of the building.

As time passed the bookkeeper taught him accounting, the stenographer shorthand and typing. Each in turn left the bank and Mr. Taber not only took on their duties but became teller, cashier, and loan officer. In September 1890 there was a threatened Indian uprising. The settlers on the prairie came into town and found shelter in homes, the school, the church, or their own wagons. Mr. Taber locked the vault, the bank, and took the bank's revolver with him. The villagers wired the governor who arrived the next day with ammunition and

76

Springfield rifles. A militia was formed and, since the captain was his prospective father-in-law, Mr. Taber joined. The federal government ordered all Indians back to the reservations. When Sitting Bull refused to return to the reservation an Indian policeman shot and killed him. This ended the uprising to the north.

The following account was written by Mr. Taber in 1952, 20 years before a book made the incident famous in our time:

> Further south, the Indians were still undecided about returning to their reservation. The federal government then sent a detachment of the regular army under General Miles to subdue them. The Indians were intimidated by this show of force. They wanted to come in but were afraid of the soldiers. They would advance and then retreat. Without the necessary patience General Miles should have had, he ordered his troops to fire. With machine guns they mowed down about a hundred Indians, a wicked and unnecessary act; the last opportunity General Miles could add to his glory. This is known as the *Battle of Wounded Knee.* Thus ended the Indian War in which I had so fearfully enlisted.

Dissatisfied with his job at the bank and convinced he must earn his living elsewhere, Mr. Taber broke away and moved to Minneapolis. Even though the enterprises which lured him there failed, his association with I. J. Eales, who became a doctor, led to the publication of Eales & Taber's "Anatomical and Physiological Chart of the Human Body." During this uncertain time Mr. Taber adopted his slogan "Nil Desperandum"—never dispair. He moved on to Chicago and eventually the Chart earned $40,000.

In order to keep going he worked in the complaint department of Montgomery Ward, became editor of a mail order catalog for a laundry machine company, then edited the first catalog for the Fair, a Chicago department store. Next he became editor of a monthly magazine *The National Progress;* from there, the literary editor of the *Chicago Daily News.* His review of an English dictionary published by Laird and Lee led them to make him an offer; he became their editor for more dictionaries.

After failing to get Bobbs-Merrill to publish his novel *Quicksand,* (about girls in the sweatshops) he published a *Dictionary for Nurses* in 1905, another mail order item that kept the family busy wrapping packages and carting them to the post office. Over a period of time, earnings from the dictionary totaled $15,000. Without income from the chart and the dictionary, life would have been very different for the Taber family.

Word of Mr. Taber's experience with dictionaries reached the G. & C. Merriam Company, who offered to make him their educational representative from Ohio eastward. Another man was hired for the west! Mr. Taber soon found out that teachers and administrators knew little about the use of dictionaries even though they had been using the Merriam-Webster for 50 years. He had to teach them diacritical markings. Funk & Wagnalls made him a better offer, but success of this dictionary was limited because of the complex system of diacritics developed by Dr. Funk. It took college level students to understand them.

Finally Mr. Taber settled down to become editor and manager of J.B. Lippincott Company's schoolbook department in Chicago. It was much of the knowledge gained here that he put to use in developing nursing textbooks for F.A. Davis. The position with Lippincott continued from 1916 to 1929. After two years of free-lance editing, during which he became associated with Davis, he moved to Philadelphia, at their invitation, to be full time textbook editor. The company had made an effort to get into the schoolbook business. However, this high volume business requires tremendous capital, a rarity in 1931. Mr. Taber's efforts were directed toward publishing nursing textbooks.

Mr. Taber claimed to be disappointed that he couldn't perform in his field of expertise, schoolbooks, even though he came with a signed contract to publish Taber's *Digest of Medical Terms.* I assume he thought he could do both. However, the presence of Mr. Jackson from the bank dictated what we could and could not do. Even so, the company refused to publish the dictionary, a testament to the struggle we suffered in the thirties. Under the threat of a serious legal battle the dictionary was published as *Taber's Cyclopedic Medical Dictionary,* an instant success.

Mr. Taber said that he became interested in dictionaries in those early years in Newark. On Sundays he was permitted to read only the Bible and the dictionary. Next his teacher in Dakota, Henry Bacon, drilled him thoroughly in the mastery of Latin and Greek roots. Bacon is the man who conspired to help Mr. Taber leave home, put him up when he returned, and helped him build a sod house all his own.

Desperate for a formal education Mr. Taber found himself frustrated by the need to survive and to provide for his family. He subscribed to the works of standard authors such as Dickens, Thackeray, and Scott and made a practice of writing a synopsis of each work as read. Laird and Lee introduced him to the editing of dictionaries. The experience of publishing the anatomical chart with Dr. Eales first interested him in medicine. The *Dictionary for Nurses* gave him a taste of being an author, and Merriam a sense of the market—what people needed in a dictionary. Lippincott provided the final touch, knowing what teachers and students needed most in textbooks. Mr. Taber and *Taber's Cyc-*

lopedic Medical Dictionary were a man and a book whose time had come. He was nearly 70 years of age.

In less than 15 years, Mr. Taber launched a medical dictionary, perhaps the best selling book of its kind, and 30 nursing textbooks which set the style for a generation. Consider his working conditions: When he arrived on the scene the company was just about to release volume one of Dr. Piersol's *Cyclopedia of Medicine, Surgery, Specialties.* Manufacturing expenses and salesmen's commissions were paid in advance and collections were made painfully by the month. The treasurer resented Mr. Taber as an unnecessary expense, the sales manager hated him as a competitor, the retail accounts manager disliked him because he was not under his control, and the man from the bank sided with the old guard. He wasn't convinced of the success of Mr. Taber's *textbooks.*

Aunt Irene and Mr. Taber loved a good fight and they had many. Both betrayed their feelings by displaying wicked smiles after each encounter. Mr. Taber remained irreverent throughout his years with Davis. He had no respect for anyone in the office except the doctors, he always referred to staff meetings as prayer meetings, and whenever he passed Dunie Wolfe at her typewriter, he winked and said, "Hi, Foxy!"

Ken Bussy called Mr. Taber "an American original."[8] I called our new building "the house that Taber built." On his ninety-seventh birthday, his last, Mr. Taber received a telegram from the American Medical Association, "Congratulations on your 97th anniversary and your great contribution to American medicine."

8. R. Kenneth Bussy: *Philadelphia's Publishers and Printers: An Informal History.* Philadelphia Book Clinic, 1976.
Also consulted: *National Cyclopedia of American Biography.* James T. White & Company, Clifton, N.J.

REFLECTIONS

From the first draft to the final manuscript of this little book I discarded as many chapters as you see here. Somewhere along the way I lost the kitchen stove. I must pay tribute to the coal range, as we called it, because it played such a vital role in our daily lives during my childhood. On the right side were three auxillary gas burners and over the stove a small and a large gas oven. These were used only under extreme conditions because to *use* gas was to *waste* gas (as we have already learned about water). A metal box on the wall held matches and a wooden box contained salt which was dispensed in pinches or handsful as needed. On the left side was a 25 gallon water tank heated by the stove. Since the tank was near the door, it was customary for everyone to put his hand on the tank as he entered the room to see how much hot water was on hand. Twenty-five gallons is not much; so no one dared take a bath in the morning and a shave with really hot water was a

83

luxury. When someone did take a bath, a trip to the kitchen was always necessary first to check if the hot water was down far enough in the tank to supply a full tub of hot water.

The small gas oven was filled with tins of crackers to keep them crisp. The large oven was an ideal place to warm the plates for dinner. It also served for quick drying of delicate hand-laundered items.

The range itself had six round lids. The two on the right were over the fire box where all the cooking was done. The stove polish there wore off quickly because of heat and constant use. The other four lids were over an air space through which heat circulated around the oven. A kettle of warm water, always on the left side of the stove, would quickly be brought to a boil by sliding it over the fire box. There were four doors on the front of the stove. One gave access to the end of the grate where a handle was applied to shake the dead ashes out of the fire box. The large one with the words "Novelty Kitchener" cast in it, was the oven door. Below that was the wood box. When that was opened Snap's head would usually pop out because it was her favorite place to sleep. To the right of the woodbox was the ash pit which had to be emptied, and just to the right of the stove under the gas burners was the scuttle which had to be filled.

The oven did not have a thermometer. Aunt Ray determined the temperature by placing her hand on the door handle: if too hot to touch, it was right for a standing roast; just very hot, poultry was the right dish; and warm, it was biscuits or corn bread. During the day when the fire was banked the oven heat was not wasted. Baked beans, rice pudding, or something was cooking slowly. There was always a time, as the temperature rose or fell, that was right for gingerbread or my favorite, oatmeal cookies.

When the furnace fire was banked, a sweater

84

was necessary in most of the house. The upper floors were always colder than the first floor. Sometimes my room seemed to be near freezing. Aunt Ray's room had the sun all day, but my room faced north and west. The kitchen was always warm and a welcome retreat from the winter cold. After skating, sledding, or just tramping in the snow, you could prop your feet on the oven door until your circulation returned to normal. At such times the dog would come out from behind the stove to be petted.

I relate this simple existence to the first meeting I attended as a member of the Board of Directors. The decision to be made was whether or not to have the office windows puttied and painted. After three hours of debate, it was decided that we would manage to get by for another winter and no action was taken in spite of the fact that the wind whistled through the spaces between the glass and sash.

The only regret I had about tearing down the old building was losing the safe. It was a large safe with double doors and the cost of removing it from the second floor was prohibitive. It had to be broken up with sledge hammers. As soon as the hammers struck, powdered alum, the fire proofing, permeated everything. Through the dust I saw the date painted on the inside of one of the doors, December 1868. In five more months it would have been 100 years old. It didn't quite make it.

Throughout my years with Davis my best friend was Wyatt H. Peterson. He was hired by Mr. Taber and was one of four educational representatives, when I started with the company, but worth more than the other three put together. Wyatt was a very positive person, always knew what he was about, and was better informed about all our books than anyone I ever met. He showed an intense loyalty to the company and the family. He accepted me immediately and in his positive way was determined that we would all succeed. I made my

first call on a customer with Wyatt. It is small wonder that I called on him when I needed a sales manager. Wyatt stayed with my children and me when my first wife died and he was best man the second time around.

At one time Wyatt's territory stretched from Washington, D.C. to El Paso, Texas. Traveling by car was very time consuming and tiring and also kept him away from home for longer periods than most people would tolerate. Finally he took flying lessons, bought a Cessna 120, and for 12 years covered his territory by plane. He was our only flying representative and perhaps the only one in book publishing.

After becoming Executive Vice President, illness forced Wyatt into early retirement. The old spirit remained with him. He got around on a motorcycle until the last of a series of coronary heart attacks took his life August 30, 1978.

Per Saugman, Chairman and Managing Director of Blackwell Scientific Publications, Ltd., wrote in a recent letter, "Your memoriam notice about Wyatt calls back endless memories of this remarkable man. He was, I think, one of the few magicians of the booktrade it has ever been my pleasure to meet. Everything he touched he did with an excitement and enthusiasm which was without parallel. The greater the challenge, the greater the fun and the greater the effort."

Then there was Miss Hynes. One day her boss told me that he started with the company in September 1909 and "she was here when I came." Actually Frances W. Hynes came to us in June 1909 right out of high school. She must hold the record for length of service with the company, 58 years. I don't recall an unpleasant word from her. She was always agreeable and hard working. An occasional card from her displayed the same firm hand that for all those years appeared on our ledger cards. While putting the finishing touches on this manuscript, I was informed of her death August 20, 1978.

The passing of Wyatt Peterson and Frances Hynes just before our one hundredth anniversary adds a note of sorrow to this history. They are symbolic of the many people who served 30, 40, and even 50 years and gave all of their energy and resources to enable the company to survive.

In retrospect: F.A. Davis was a country school teacher who wouldn't remain satisfied. He came to the city and began fulfilling his desires as a book salesman. When he was handed a manuscript he became a publisher, and when he read about the "healthiest spot on earth" he set out to make it a health resort for the millions. He wasn't allowed enough time to finish his mission but many who followed him benefited from his efforts. I was raised to believe that there is a hallowed place for such persons.

With tenacity and grit Aunt Irene enabled the F.A. Davis Company to survive bankruptcy and the Great Depression. She was able to attract a man of Dr. Piersol's caliber and high standing to take over where Dr. Sajous left off. She answered a "situations wanted" ad in *Publishers Weekly* and found a Clarence W. Taber who wanted to be identified with a publisher. In him she saw the means to develop our publishing in nursing. His success with *Taber's Cyclopedic Medical Dictionary* was, I'm sure, beyond his most ambitious dreams. After World War II she doggedly carried on, waiting until Bobby was ready. She came to the office four days a week until she was 85; then she cut back to three days a week. I don't think she was willing to die until she felt it was all right to go.

And what have I added to all this? Well, first I put up storm sash to keep the windows and frames from falling out. By the time we put tile on the floor and ceiling, threw out all the plants that had rotted the window

88

sills, put in window air conditioners, carpeted the private offices, replaced the furniture, and brought the rest rooms up to minimum standards (we never did get heat in them), we had blue prints on our new building—our first move in about 75 years.

My knottiest problem was resolving the fate of the *Cyclopedia of Medicine, Surgery, Specialties.* Progress in medicine had made it obsolete and we had to let it go out of print. This one item represented half our sales volume at the time and the prospect of finding new product to replace it without sinking into oblivion was awesome. We tried everything we could think of. In our worst years the sales never went below a one digit percentage figure. Every year in this last decade we set a record for sales volume.

Because Aunt Irene held on so long we did not grow when other publishers experienced their greatest growth. I felt we needed long-term financing to catch up. With our treasurer, I pounded the pavements of Philadelphia and New York to find someone who had faith in us. We were refused by everyone; so we set our sights much lower and grew at a slower pace with short-term borrowing. Today our line of credit is more than we need and adequate for the most ambitious project we could conceive.

Financial sources all look for the same things whether it is a bank, factor, investment banker, investment broker, or the man on the street. After performance they want young management and designated replacements for key people. I have watched the average age of management decline from 65 to about 40. At 56, I'm now the "old man." Succession within the company is planned and while plans don't always materialize to the letter, one is better than none at all.

Not everything shows up on balance sheets and profit and loss statements. In my time two women died at their desks. It reminded me of that ghostly

89

photograph of a graveyard with the caption, "Our Retirement Plan." Luckily I have been able to arrange a plan, even though some or all of it comes out of profits.

Recently I spent time in the mountains of North Carolina, which helped me resolve this story. One morning at breakfast I sat looking out at Rock Mountain, unspoiled and standing proud, weathered, and independent. I saw its reflection upside down in the lake and the ripples in the water caused by the wind made it appear less perfect than it is. Behind the mountain the sun was rising on a new, crisp, inspiring day.

LIFE SHORTENING HABITS

BY

ARNOLD LORAND, M.D.

Carlsbad, Czecho-Slovakia

CONTENTS

The Ten Chief Life Shortening Habits

PHILADELPHIA

F. A. DAVIS COMPANY, PUBLISHERS

1924